Consciousness and Mind

Consciousness and Mind

Mark Rozen Pettinelli

CONTENTS

2 | 2 23

1

An emotional experience involves:
  A perception
The valence of the feeling (positive or negative feeling)
1st person point of view or perspective
An Evaluation
Thoughts about the emotion or judgments
Motivational feelings (whether positive or negative motivation)
Unconscious or conscious thoughts, feelings or behaviors
The function of a feeling is to motivate us in some way

In conclusion of my research, in order to understand what you are feeling, simply try to feel what you can feel. It is simple, I could just try to figure out what I am feeling at the moment. I can try to analyze my feelings using what I learned about feelings. So then what would I use to analyze or understand my feelings then. I know about the mental processes, the main ones are feeling, thought, attention, perception, awareness, language, and memory. So I could say to myself, well now I'm feeling this and that, the feeling feels like this and this or that mental process is being used. If you don't know what the mental processes are you could look them up or just think about how your mind is working and what it could possibly be doing at the moment to produce the feelings your currently experiencing. That is my guide for understanding what you are feeling at any time or the current moment. You could just ask yourself, "what mental processes could my mind be using in order to make myself feel this way. Then you

could try to figure out how you are feeling and ask a different question, "what am I feeling right now, how did it get this way, and what mental processes are being used."

An emotional or cognitive experience. But what does that mean? I mean, what exactly is an emotional experience, and how does it compare to a cognitive experience? I suppose somethings are intellectual while others are just feelings or emotions. They can be combined also, I don't know how it works exactly but it seems like there can be feelings and thoughts, or intellectual feelings and non-intellectual feelings all mixing in and combining in an experience.

What else is there anyway/ There is thoughts and consciousness, and attention and consciousness, i said before, you could be aware of any of your mental processes.

Some points on consciousness

If consciousness becomes more powerful, it might need more stimulation probably because it's just larger so it needs more stuff, even though it has more power. A neurologist in 2004 - Michele Maci - pointed out to me that I didn't have that much anxiety when I was in high school or when i was a kid. I took that to mean recently that although my consciousness was more powerful, i had more anxiety then when my mind was simple. The more powerful consciousness must need more stuff for some reason, i had huge problems with anxiety after I graduated from high school in 2003.

Another point is about cognitive psychology or how the mind works. If it works from basic mental processes like thinking, feeling, perception, language, memory and attention and other mental processes, then why would the mind be that complicated. This just seems like a simple understanding of how the mind functions, also people can become conscious of their feelings or thoughts, and have a stronger consciousness. Do I need to explain what I mean by a stronger consciousness then? It is hard to explain, I would think children have a weaker consciousness than adults, at least mine was much weaker than it is now than when I was a child.

People can be conscious of their thoughts and their feelings. I would think that as the mind becomes more powerful, the person's consciousness would need to understand the feelings and thoughts that it has or they would be confused or go crazy. The feelings and thoughts could become more powerful, and as this happens the mind would need to understand what those feelings and thoughts are.

So if there is a stimulus or trigger, the person then experiences feelings, and they can also think about those feelings with thoughts. So is there a trigger, then a feeling or a thought, or is there an intellectual experience and an emotional experience? The emotional experience would involve feelings, while the intellectual experience would involve thoughts. I mean, what is going on in any emotional experience? It could be intellectual and involve thoughts, or it could be emotional and involve feelings, or it could be both intellectual and emotional at the same time, and involve the experience of feelings and thoughts at the same time.

My consciousness is a lot stronger than it was when I was a child, it actually gradually got stronger in my 20's and 30's and now I also have more powerful emotions. I think that's how humans have evolved, to have stronger emotions and feelings. I already pointed out that meant that I have to be more aware or understanding of my feelings and thoughts because my consciousness is more powerful.

I mean think about it, if there is a powerful consciousness then that means there can be other people or a previous state that had a more simple consciousness. What do I mean by a more powerful consciousness anyway? I pointed out that it would have a harder time understanding more powerful feelings and thoughts. And would need to understand those feelings and thoughts so it wouldn't be confused.

But I mean, what then is the difference between an intellectual experience and an emotional experience? SO what is going on then. In any experience, there are thoughts and feelings, but it's more complicated than that I suppose. I mean, what is going on with an intellectual experience and an emotional experience then? I suppose it's pretty simple, it's mostly just the person experiencing feelings and having thoughts.

I don't know what else to add to that, an experience is an experience, it involves both feelings and thoughts, but is there anything more to add to that explanation?

So what else do I need to figure out? These are my final notes that I won't include in my book. I don't know what else I might need to learn. Um, so I think I know everything I need to know in order to function. I don't think I need to know anything else. I can think clearly and logically and can function. So I'm really excited, other people are conscious. I'm still going through some books. I'll add the information that I learn here. I don't know if there's anything else I need to learn. I mean, what else would I need to know? I can function fine, I don't even know if I already said that. Now I'm being guided, but I wrote that final book by myself. These are notes about other stuff I would want to learn. That makes sense, they didn't have the academics figured out until I finished explaining some academics. I was providing a critical contribution to the academics that they needed for a long time and to finally finish the academics. I don't know what the other people who were contributing to the academics had to offer, but I was part of the small number of people who were contributing to the academics and working together with other academics to figure everything out. I don't know what they're trying to research now, my part in that is over. One of my final ideas was that thought is different from feeling. Feelings and thoughts can also influence each other. Now I keep track of my feelings and my thoughts so I can be intelligent, conscious and logical. I've always been logical and clear thinking but I wasn't that smart before I did all this research over the last decade. So I'm just going to post here what else I might need or can learn that I think might be valuable information, but I'm being guided so it won't be posted as part of my last book "THe selected writings of Mark Pettinelli". SO I don't know what else I might need to know, I'm still reading books and thinking about stuff. My last insight was that people think and feel at the same time, and they can keep track of those feelings and thoughts. It's important to note that people can think and feel at the same time. They can also keep track of those feelings and thoughts, and if feelings lead to thoughts and if thoughts lead to feelings. Um so what else would I need to know? It's kind of important to keep track of your feelings and thoughts. I don't know if there's anything else I need to learn then. Maybe I'm just done with the research. I mean, if I can keep track of my feelings and thoughts and can function in a practical manner, and think clearly and logically, then I don't know what else I would need to achieve.

I'm functioning perfectly fine right now. I keep track of my feelings and thoughts and how I'm doing in general. I can think clearly and logically, so all that works. Um, so I need to think more about that. I wrote a lot about the difference between feelings and emotions. I concluded that the mix of feelings that people feel can be complicated, and that there is no set definition between the difference of feelings and emotions, that it is kind of subjective and can be defined in various ways, the important part just being how the person feels, whatever their feelings or emotions or thoughts are doing at that time. Um so that seems like a pretty good explanation. I don't know what else I would need to figure out or analyze. Consciousness is important. There might be information about consciousness that I might need to learn or research. I don't know what else I might need to know. I understand how the mind thinks about stuff, that seems like a good understanding. I also understand how the mind feels, the mind feels emotions and feelings all the time. Um so i don't know what else i might need to figure out. It seems like I know everything that I need to understand. I mean I know about the mental processes and I know about thinking and feeling. There is also perception, memory, language, judgment and reasoning and choice, learning, attention and awareness, categories, knowledge, mental representations and concepts, problem solving and decision making.and creativity, automaticity, insight and self knowledge. Um so what else would I need to understand about consciousness or feelings and how they function in the mind? I mean I understand how feelings work and I understand how consciousness works. Consciousness is all the mental processes working together to form a picture of how the mind functions. THen the person becomes conscious of their feelings and thoughts and other mental functions. So feelings and thoughts contribute to the persons consciousness. I mean, what is it to say that the person is conscious anyway? I mean I guess it's just awareness right. Attention and awareness are 2 of the mind's mental processes.

So what exactly is consciousness? Being conscious and aware I guess. Conscious means aware I would think, so if someone is conscious it means that they are aware of themselves or their environment or their mind. Um so what else do i need to understand in order to function? I mean I can feel my emotions and my feelings and know when I am thinking. Is there anything else I would need to know? I mean, what else is there behind understanding consciousness? I guess I would have to keep track of all of my feelings and thoughts to be aware in general. If I do that then I think I should be pretty good and well off. I mean i think I just need to do that, keep track of my feelings and thoughts and behaviors. Seems pretty simple. I mean, I don't know the biology of it but still understand how it works.

Consciousness can be pretty complicated, for instance what is consciousness, what does it feels like to feel something? I mean I guess consciousness is just the sum total of our mental processes. So consciousness is just the combination of our attention and awareness, sometimes our memory and sometimes we use our language. It is also the combination of our thoughts and our feelings, whatever it is we are feeling at the moment and if we are thinking about something. I mean, thought and feeling are probably the two greatest contributions to consciousness. What else could be going on other than thinking about something and feeling something? We could also be more or less aware and attentive. We could be using our judgment or making decisions or problem solving. What are some of the other mental processes that our consciousness could be using? We could be learning something, We could be trying to figure something out or problem solve.

So consciousness is just basically what we are aware of, or if we are aware in general. A lot of things contribute to our awareness or our consciousness, like whatever we are aware of at any moment. Humans are aware of their thoughts and feelings and other mental functions like memory and attention and awareness, language and knowledge and concepts, their thinking processes and feeling processes, so whatever they are feeling they could be aware of.

What else is there to understanding consciousness? Someone could have a thought, that would make them aware of whatever the thought is about right. Feelings can also be about stuff, for instance if you feel happy there might be a reason you feel that way. What else is complicated about feelings and thoughts, i previously said that feelings and thoughts make a person more conscious right. Feelings and thoughts can be caused by something or be connected to something, like a behavior or another feeling or thought. That's important for consciousness if you think about it because our feelings and thoughts help make us more aware. But what then is consciousness? Consciousness is our awareness of our feelings and thoughts and other mental processes. If a person is aware of their feelings and thoughts then they are conscious right. If someone is having feelings and thoughts then the person could be a conscious person, but they wouldn't be as conscious as someone who is aware of their feelings and thoughts.

I mean, so what is consciousness then? How aware a person is of their environment or their mind. In order for someone to be aware of their mind or environment they would have to be aware of their mental processes like feelings and thoughts. Those are probably the two most significant mental processes. So how aware someone is of their feelings and thoughts makes the person more conscious and aware. It makes them aware of what they are feeling and thinking, and their other mental processes like language, memory, attention and awareness. So someone could be aware of how aware they are, or if they are using language or speaking, or using their memory. If a person is aware of any of that stuff then they would be more aware of what their mind is doing. A person could also be aware of what is going on in their environment.

A person could be aware of what they are thinking about also, the more aware they are of what they are thinking about the more conscious they would be because they would be aware of their own mind and their environment.

I need to simplify that. Consciousness is a persons awareness of their mind or their environment. So if someone is aware of what their mind is doing then they would be more conscious. They could also be aware of their environment, the environment could be influencing or causing the person's mind to feel or think things. So what is consciousness then? A person could be conscious of their mind and what it is doing. It could be experiencing any of the mental processes such as attention, awareness, memory, learning, language, feeling, thinking, problem solving, decision making, perception, insight, creativity, knowledge, concepts, mental representations, the use of categories, or other mental processes. all of those mental processes are things the mind does. So consciousness would be if someone is aware of what their mind is doing. One thing a mind could be doing is experiencing the mental processes I just listed.

A person could be aware of what they are feeling or thinking or whatever it is they are experiencing. That makes them more conscious because it is what they are experiencing or feeling. Most of the mental processes contribute to the persons feelings or thoughts. A person could be aware of what they are feeling. just feeling something is different from being aware of those feelings. It could be that someone has a feeling that they are not aware of. I guess that could involve various degrees of awareness.

that seems complicated, for instance what does it mean to be aware of a feeling or thought or aware of something in the real world? that is actually pretty simple, it is just how aware someone is of what they are feeling or thinking, or whatever else their mind might be doing.

The mind can also experience things from their environment, but those things get experienced in the mind.

That seems like a more simple explanation of consciousness. Consciousness is just the awareness of a persons feelings and thoughts and other things the mind can do or experience.

That seems like a pretty good explanation of consciousness. Either someone is feeling something or thinking about something, and they can be aware of what they are thinking or feeling. Whatever the person's mind is doing they could be aware of. For instance they could be aware of a feeling that they are having. They could be aware of thoughts that they are having. If they are trying to figure something out then they know they are doing that. They could also know about the feelings that they are having at any moment. I can feel things right now and I'm aware of those feelings. I'm aware that I have feelings and thoughts. I am perfectly aware of my feelings and how I feel all the time or just in general.

So I'm going through a lot of material. There are feelings and thoughts in the mind. I can think clearly, and I can function, what else would I need to be able to do anyway? Thinking is pretty simple if you think about it, I mean, a thought is just a thought, and a feeling is just a feeling. Feelings and thoughts come and go in the mind all of the time. What else does the mind do anyway? That enables me to function and think clearly. I am logical and can think clearly. There's an emotional experience and an intellectual experience that I can feel. THe emotional experience involves feelings while the intellectual experience involves thoughts. Thoughts are important for thinking, while feelings help people have experiences of feeling. So there is a feeling that someone feels, is the feeling physical or is it only a mental feeling? I mean, there is a mental or psychological world and a physical world that can both experience feelings. Are feelings physical or are they mental then? That's kind of a complicated question then. I want to know what all my feelings are and how they feel exactly right. I don't know if there is a lot to understand about how feelings feel. I mean, what is complicated about feeling stuff.

It seems like it's pretty simple I would think. I'm trying to do an analysis of what my feelings feel like. There are physical feelings and mental feelings. I guess there's a big difference between mental feelings and physical feelings then. Consciousness is important for feelings, feelings can be conscious. How could a feeling be unconscious then? If it is unconscious then you wouldn't feel it right, so it wouldn't even be a feeling. How can anything be unconscious then if unconscious means by definition that it is beneath your awareness. How can I separate out mental feelings from physical feelings then, I mean, when i feel a physical feeling it is also mental because i can feel it in my brain or feel it. I mean, all physical feelings are processed in the brain, which is where everything is felt, both mental and physical feelings are felt in the brain. What then is the difference between a physical feeling and a mental feeling then? I suppose that physical feelings feel physical while mental feelings you don't feel a physical presence. That means you can feel physical feelings People can also feel mental feelings, those feelings don't have a physical presence like how physical feelings do. Physical feelings you can feel somewhere in your body, while mental feelings do not have a physical presence. So what else would I need to know, I know that there are sensory feelings, but aren't all physical feelings sensory ones? Like taste and touch, those are both physical feelings. So that means that some things feel physical, while others are mental and do not have a physical presence. That is kind of obvious. What else would I need to know about feelings and thoughts then. So i don't know what else to say, i have feelings and thoughts and stuff. I don't need to explain anymore of it. Actually I explained a lot in my previous articles about it.

So what else do I need to learn? What else is there to learn anyway, I mean I know what the definition of consciousness is, I also know that I have feelings and thoughts.

So what else do I need to learn or take notes about? There's feelings and thoughts, there are also physical sensations. They used to be doing research, I had a role to play in that. Now everything is figured out and stuff. What else is there to take notes about? I took notes about feelings and thoughts. For instance some feelings could be somewhat unconscious. Thoughts can influence feelings. How could a feeling influence a thought? If you have a feeling, then you think about the feeling and come up with a thought I suppose.

So what else do I need to figure out anyway? I understand how the mind works. There's feelings and thoughts, that's mostly what the mind does.

There's also mental processes like problem solving and decision making, attention and awareness, judgment, reasoning and choice, memory, learning and language, mental representations, knowledge, concepts and categories, automaticity, self-knowledge and insight, creativity and perception. That's pretty much all of the mental processes Consciousness isn't really a mental process, well I guess it is, but it is more like the combination of all the mental processes. So feelings can influence thoughts and thoughts can influence feelings. When would someone think about a feeling then? Or how could a thought influence a feeling? When do feelings influence thoughts and when do thoughts influence feelings? So feelings can influence thinking, and thinking or thoughts can influence how a person is feeling. So what is the difference between feelings and thinking then? I think that thinking is intellectual, while feelings are emotional.

So I'm trying to figure this out, do I even need to make any more progress? I mean, I'm pretty developed physically and intellectually, I don't know if I need to get any smarter or stronger. I figured out the difference between feelings and thoughts.

I'm trying to do an analysis here. What else do I need to figure out anyway? I guess that there's a lot of information I could benefit from learning about. I could try to do that I suppose.

What would I need to learn though? I already know basically how the mind works and how feelings and thoughts work. That seems like a pretty good understanding.

Is there anything else about the mind to understand other than that it has feelings and thoughts? What else does the mind do? It categorizes information and knowledge. It thinks about different concepts with thoughts,

What else is there anyway/ There is thoughts and consciousness, and attention and consciousness, i said before, you could be aware of any of your mental processes.

States of consciousness Representations Mental states

So what else am I supposed to learn about consciousness? There is awareness of your own mind and your environment. What is everything that someone might be aware of anyway?

Consciousness can be pretty complicated if you think about it, i mean, what exactly is going on in the brain that makes consciousness form?

So what could be complicated about consciousness? There are the mental processes like attention, memory, learning, language, judgment, reasoning, choice, automaticity, self-knowledge, insight, thinking, feeling, knowledge, mental representations, concepts, categories, problem solving, decision making, thinking, feeling, perception and creativity.

So that's how the mind works basically, by using those mental processes, and someone could be more or less aware of what their mind is doing and what processes are being used. They could also be aware of external inputs from their environment through their senses. So that is external inputs and internal inputs that they could be aware of. I mean, what else is there to understanding consciousness anyway? Seems pretty simple, you can just be aware of what your mind is doing and what it's processing.

So what does it mean to be aware anyway? You can be aware in general or aware of a mental process, or aware of something external like an input from the environment. I mean, when someone is aware of something then they understand what it is they are thinking and feeling then they become more aware of it I suppose. But what then does it mean to be 'aware' of something then?

1 Consciousness is complicated

2 Energy is complicated (there's global energy and interpersonal energy)

3 Logic can be difficult to acquire (psychosis is serious)

4 Cognitive psychology is difficult to understand

5 Global energy is complicated you need to have a feeling for it

6 Consciousness can be isolated and influenced by energy or other types of stimulation (medication, drugs and food for instance)

7 If the consciousness is isolated then what does it need to support it? I said it can be influenced by energy and other types of stimulation, but that can be complicated for instance how could the consciousness function without any support? Can you get a feeling for that for instance? I can, I basically try to feel what my consciousness would be like without getting any inputs and by itself, I can get a feeling for that. That's pretty interesting. Like how would my consciousness be if it was by itself not getting any inputs?

I think three things are needed to continue to develop earth until the development is complete and everything repeats 1. Biological development 2. Technological development 3. Psychological development

Eventually those could be completely developed, The biological development includes the development of biotech, which is a combination of two of those things (obviously biology and technology). Also, everything will eventually be repeating because there is only a limited number of ideas or categories or things people can do, the technological and mental development will also eventually be finished. They could change things up I guess but the mental development will be finished, I pointed out that at the beginning of time the consciousness, feelings and thoughts people had were much weaker than now.

I'm good at 5 academic subjects, 1) logic 2) cognitive psychology 3) consciousness 4) the mind 5) emotion and cognition, those subjects are also obviously related So what do i understand about those topics. Cognitive psychology is important because it's mostly about the minds mental processes. i listed those earlier. i mean, just talking about the mind's mental processes demonstrates how the mind functions. what else would someone need to know about how the mind works and is structured. Is there a difference between how it is structured and how it functions, however? How it functions would just be the behaviors and outputs it has like the actions it tells the body and mind to do. while how it is structured would be how thinking works in the mind, or how executive functioning and emotion regulation function in the mind anyway.

So there are feelings and thoughts, and then there is your awareness of your feelings and thoughts. Awareness can also be described as consciousness, you can be conscious of your feelings and thoughts and your other mental processes like memory, attention, language, judgement and reasoning.

What else could someone be conscious of in their own mind then. I mean, obviously they could be conscious of their external environment or conscious of other mental processes. You could be conscious of your perceptions, like your perception of your external environment or your perception of your own internal feelings and thoughts.

If I want to learn anything that I want to, what would i need to study, I mean there are a lot of topics out there, there are sciences that use math and science that do not a good understanding at all.

Cognitive psychology The mind being dependent on stimulation and what it would be like to be without any inputs into the mind or an isolated consciousness The energy on the planet part of which provides stimulation for the mind Logic and points about logic Cognitive psychology and points about it like feelings and thoughts and a simplified version of how the mental processes work Maintaining clear and logical thinking and developing intellect and physical ability is complicated A feeling for life on the planet (kind of similar to the point about the energy on the planet)

So there's consciousness, and there's energy inputs into the consciousness. you can isolate the consciousness and figure out what all the inputs are that are going into it. it is supported by different kinds of energy and stimulation. what is the difference between medication and other types of energy then?

There's an isolated consciousness in the brain right. The consciousness can be influenced by energy, what does that mean exactly, if you feel cold, then that impacts your consciousness, you can feel the cold. it influences your feelings, then maybe you feel bad because you are cold. what is the difference between feeling bad that you are cold and just feeling bad at other times then? those are all different aspects of consciousness. Some feelings are powerful while others are weak. For instance if you feel very cold then you are probably going to feel very bad, your consciousness gets effected by the feelings.

What does that mean, that your consciousness can be effected by your feelings? I think that your consciousness is basically who you are, it is your identity and sense of self. This consciousness of who you are can be effected by different feelings and types of energy, or lack of energy. if you are not getting any energy inputs into your consciousness then you might feel bad and you could suffer. Your consciousness would suffer or you would suffer, saying the person is sad is the same as saying that their consciousness is sad, and so on.

So there is energy inputs into the consciousness. What does that mean exactly anyway? What could be an input for the person or their mind or their consciousness. The temperature influences the person right. What else influences how a person is feeling, that's kind of important to note.

Lot's of things can influence how a person is feeling. How does medication influence how a person is feeling then? It could alter thoughts or feelings. But i mean, lots of things change people's feelings and thoughts, not just medications.

So what are all the energy inputs that could be influencing the consciousness then? What is the complete picture, in other words, of how the consciousness functions? There's an isolated consciousness in the brain right, it gets support from stimulation and different types of energy, what are all of those inputs?

Furthermore, the consciousness might be completely unsupported, then it would probably be about to die right, that would be an example of what the consciousness would be like without any inputs, I would think that it would always need inputs. I suppose a person could be fine without stimulation for a while, but there would still be energy inputs going into the consciousness from their body or brain.

So how does all of this work? There are inputs from the environment that our senses gather, like taste, touch, sight, sound and smell. Then our mind processes the inputs and feels what they cause it to feel. That causes the mind to experience the feelings that the inputs cause. For instance, if you see something red you might experience an emotion because of that color, some of the feelings could be physical feelings, while other feelings might be more psychological. For instance, if you see a hot girl, you might feel aroused. Those are physical feelings resulting from the sensory input of sight and maybe touch (even though you might not actually be touching the girl).

So what else is there to the picture? People feel physical and mental feelings resulting from the sensory inputs all of the time. Mental feelings might include emotions or other feelings, while physical feelings might include a bunch of different kinds of feeling like feeling cold or warm, or full or hungry.

So what else is there to cognitive psychology anyway? There's emotion and cognition and the mental processes, there are other mental processes other than feeling and thought then. What is so complicated about that though? I wouldn't think anything complicated is going on it seems. It's mostly just feelings and thoughts i would say, how complicated is that? I guess there is more going on other than that i suppose. I'll post here what else i learn then. I mean, what could be important about how the mind works other than understanding that it has feelings and thoughts and potentially other things going on. I can function perfectly fine with that understanding i think.

Consciousness is what we are aware of, if i understand something then i am aware of that understanding, for instance. it is anything that we are aware of actually. I mean, think about it, if you feel something or think about something or become aware of something by some other method- i don't think there is any other method actually. Then that is all that consciousness is. How can someone become aware of something then anyway? You can think about something or you can understand or feel a feeling. That makes you aware of the thought or the feeling. It is just about awareness then, how would I define awareness then? Aware by definition means that you understand, experience or feel something to a higher degree. You are more 'aware' of it. That is all consciousness is, being more aware of whatever it is you want to be aware of, your mind, your environment, or other things like thoughts and feelings in your mind, or different parts of your environment.

I mean, think about it, consciousness is our total awareness. To be conscious of something is to be aware of it. So someone can be conscious of their own mind, or aware of their own mind, or conscious of their environment or different things in their environment. What is total consciousness then? I suppose that would be everything a person is aware of then. I mean, what is a functioning mental state or state of consciousness?

A state of consciousness could be a mental state that means someone is aware of whatever it is they are aware of, that seems obvious, I mean, awareness is important. What is different between the word 'aware' and the word 'conscious' then? If you are conscious of something, then you are aware of it, and if you are aware of something, then you are also conscious of it. So does 'consciousness' basically mean 'awareness' then?

So what is consciousness then? Consciousness is a mind or the mind within a brain, or the state an isolated consciousness in the brain can be in, it can be in a state of consciousness. One state could be unconscious, or conscious or conscious and hallucinating.

The mind is everything that goes on in someone's mind then. That is obvious, a person can be conscious and have a mind. Their mind is their consciousness, the definition of 'mind' and 'consciousness' is similar then.

So it is clear what consciousness is then, it is an isolated person or being in the brain. It is the person's 'self' in other words, it is who they are. The consciousness works with and controls the person's brain. How does that work exactly then? If i feel happy, then my consciousness is happy and i can feel that, my brain is also interconnected to my consciousness and my brain helps myself or my consciousness be happy or function.

So what have I learned from this analysis so far. i think consciousness is clearly important to understand, because it is who we are and how we function obviously. Our brans use our consciousness all the time. I defined what a brain or consciousness might do or experience or live through. There are mental processes that are functions the mind performs.

I also pointed out that there is intellectual processing versus emotional processing. There are two different ways of experiencing the world, basically, one is intellectual and the other is emotional or physical. So how does that work then. I pointed out that there are feelings and thoughts, and that thoughts normally contribute to intellectual stimulation or feeling or understanding or processing. What does feeling contribute to in the mind then?

Feelings could contribute to some of the other mental processes, feelings can influence thoughts or thinking, they could influence learning or language processing. What else do feelings do. There can be physical feelings obviously, do those feelings become mental feelings or do they become intellectual? How would that work? I'm just trying to put some of the ideas in this page together.

Summary and further points

So if they're trying to figure out all of the academics, then what would they need to do? There are a lot of different subjects to study. The key subject i'm interested in is emotion and cognition, which i think is part of the subject of cognitive psychology. Consciousness is also a cognitive psychology topic. The topics in cognitive psychology are basically the minds mental processes i think. So what is key about the topic of emotion and cognition then anyway? My articles on google scholar (you can just enter my name in google scholar to find them, Mark Pettinelli), all talk about emotion and cognition and similar ideas or topics. So what is there to point out about emotion and cognition, or feeling and thought?, um so i think i already pointed out all of that stuff, feelings are different from thoughts, feelings are emotional processing while thoughts are intellectual processing, whatever that means anyway. Um so that is all there is to the entire topic of emotion and cognition i think. There is feeling and thinking, that's mostly what the mind does anyway, i mean i'm trying to just keep track of the significant factors here. When the mind thinks, it can feel things also, it can feel things and think about things, basically. What else is going on in the mind then anyway? I mean, i feel stuff and i think about other stuff. Or i feel things and i can think about other things then. Feelings are great because they can be pleasant or pleasurable, while thoughts are intellectual and can be about things.

So there is just three points: 1) Consciousness 2) Emotion and cognition 3) Logic

Those three points are all everything someone might need to know in order to function I think, i mean if they know how they think and feel, if they know how to think logically, and if they know how to be conscious and aware of their feelings and thoughts and themselves then they should be fine I guess. Consciousness basically means 'awareness', emotion and cognition just means that people have feelings and thoughts at the same time that they can feel or think about, and logic is obviously just thinking accurately or without bias.

So what else would i need to add to this article? i know how to function, and pointed out that the three main points are 1) consciousness 2) feelings and thoughts and 3) logic. I mean, think about it, everything someone might need to know would be how to think clearly and intelligently right. they also might need to know if they are aware of their feelings and thoughts, that's also important.

There is clear thinking, then there is intelligent thinking. what are all the different types of intelligent thinking then? You could think about different subjects, but does that really cover the basic ways of thinking then? Not really, i would think that in order to describe the basic ways of thinking I could just separate them out into the different types of thinking. There is unconscious thinking, thinking using memories, there is also stupid thinking and intelligent thinking. furthermore, there is stupid and intelligent feeling also, i already pointed that out.

So there's different kinds of information that someone can think about. There is:
1) Mathematical thinking
2) Scientific thinking
3) Clear thinking
4) Unconscious thinking
5) Thinking about memories
6) Thinking from impulses
7) Logical thinking
8) Thinking about concepts
9) Conscious thinking, is logical thinking conscious then? what is the difference between logical thinking and unconscious thinking then? i would think that needs to be clarified. Dreams are illogical usually, they are unconscious by definition. Unconscious thinking, what is that exactly anyway? Thinking that you're not fully aware of or something. That seems complicated and difficult to understand. What am i outlining what needs to be figured out then? What is the difference between emotions, thinking, clear thinking, logical thinking and unconscious

thinking? It would seem emotions can cloud thinking and be unconscious and illogical, all of those factors mix and need to be outlined.

Final analysis

so what else do people get from reading my articles then? There are feelings and thoughts, that's important but it's obvious if I just say 'there's only feelings and thoughts'. i mean, more needs to be explained about feelings and thoughts. i already mentioned that they are a part of how the mind functions, they perform in the mind with other mental processes and functions. There is also intellectual feelings and stupid feelings, stupid feelings can be physical or emotional, while intellectual feelings could be thoughts or ideas or just a stream of thought or concepts.

There is also intellectual processing and emotional processing, i mean if you think about a stream of thought is probably going to be intellectual processing while feelings of any sort is going to be some sort of processing of feelings.

So i made my specialty figuring out everything, i've been researching and studying that for a long time. For instance therapists have a practical understanding that is important for people to help them think and function in life, I would think that that is important information. Cognitive psychology is also important, for instance that holds the keys to figuring out how the mind works right. Cognitive psychology is about the mind's mental processes, there's only a few significant ones anyway, there is memory, attention, awareness, thinking, feeling, perception and language. That is how the mind thinks and performs anyway. What else would i need to explain about how the mind works then?

1) Logic

What about logic do people need to understand, I already pointed out that there is a difference between inaccurate thinking and biased thinking. People have belief systems and are illogical, I have autism and don't have very many emotions, people have always had emotions but they didn't really use to interfere with their functioning as much as they do now because now the feelings and thoughts that people have are much more powerful.

2) Cognitive Psychology

What is there to understand about cognitive psychology then? I already pointed out that there is basic functioning right. People need to be logical, understand that they have feelings and thoughts, and that they can be aware of those feelings and thoughts to different degrees. THat's the same three points I brought up earlier, 1) logic 2) emotion and cognition and 3) consciousness.

Further Points

So what else is there to understanding how the mind functions then? THere are feelings and thoughts, those determine the persons emotional and cognitive experiences. There is also how aware someone is of their feelings and thoughts, that is how conscious someone is of their thoughts and feelings or just how conscious the person is in general.

I mean, a person can be aware of what they are experiencing, that is obvious. What does that mean exactly though? What is the definition of the word 'awareness', and how does it effect understanding of how a person is feeling. A human or animal even can be aware of what they are feeling then. THere is a difference between having feelings, and understanding and being aware of those feelings.

I guess the question then is, how can someone have a feeling without being aware of it? That feeling could be considered to be unconscious or beneath the persons awareness. What does that mean though? Feelings are experiences of feeling, they feel 'like' something. THey are also strong or weak. SO then I suppose feelings either have a certain way of feeling, and can be felt to different degrees.

References

McLaughlin, B., Beckermann, A., & Walter, S. (2011). The Oxford Handbook of Philosophy of Mind. OUP Oxford.

Power, M. J., & Dalgleish, T. (2015). Cognition and emotion: From Order to Disorder. Psychology Press.

Robinson, M. D., Watkins, E. R., & Harmon-Jones, E. (2013). Handbook of Cognition and Emotion. Guilford Press.

Gensler, H. J. (2016). Introduction to logic. Routledge.

Graziano, M. S. A. (2019). Rethinking consciousness: A Scientific Theory of Subjective Experience. National Geographic Books.

Eysenck, M. W., & Keane, M. T. (2015). Cognitive Psychology: A Student's Handbook. Psychology Press.

www.ingramcontent.com/pod-product-compliance
Lightning Source LLC
Chambersburg PA
CBHW051555010526
44118CB00022B/2722